# At the CORNER of the EYE

Editors:

Naomi Long Madgett

Terry Blackhawk

Darryl Holmes

Paulette Childress White

# At the Corner of the Eye

POEMS BY
PATRICIA HOOPER

Michigan State University Press
East Lansing

All Michigan State University Press books are produced on paper which meets the requirements of American National Standard of Information Sciences—Permanence of paper for printed materials ANSI Z39.48-1984.

Michigan State University Press
East Lansing, Michigan 48823-5202

03  02  01  00  99  98  97   1  2  3  4  5  6  7  8  9

Library of Congress Cataloging-in-Publication Data


Library of Congress Cataloging-in-Publication Data

Hooper, Patricia, 1941-
    At the corner of the eye : poems / by Patricia Hooper.
    p.  cm. — (Lotus poetry series)
    ISBN 0-87013-467-1 (alk. paper)
    I. Title.  II. Series.
PS3558.059A9  1997
811'.54—dc21                                                   97-8746
                                                              CIP


Lotus Poetry Series Editor: Naomi Long Madgett

# Acknowledgments

Grateful acknowledgment is made to the editors of the following magazines, in which many of these poems first appeared: *The American Poetry Review, The American Scholar* ("Reunion"), *Blue Unicorn, The Bridge, Cincinnati Poetry Review, Green River Review, The Hudson Review* ("The Best Hour"), *The Literary Review, Midwest Quarterly, The New Criterion, Passages North, Pivot, Ploughshares* ("In the Backyard"), *Prairie Schooner, River Styx, Snowy Egret, Spectrum, Sycamore Review, The William and Mary Review,* and *Yankee.* "Annunciations" first appeared in *Poetry,* © 1993, The Modern Poetry Association.

Several poems were originally printed in *Heart of the Flower: Poems for the Sensuous Gardener,* edited by Sondra Zeidenstein, Chicory Blue Press, 1991, and in *The Flowering Trees,* by Patricia Hooper, State Street Press Chapbooks, 1995.

The author also wishes to thank Mitzi Alvin, Dan Minock, Gay Rubin, and Lorene Erickson.

*For John*

## Psalm in January

Praise to the crows who blackened
my window this morning, screaming
and calling until I looked;
to the red squirrel as it hurried
from its place under the feeder
to tremble beneath the woodpile;
to the cardinals sent flying
into the cedar branches;
to the sun, for it shone clearly
the moment I looked out

and saw from my upstairs window
the hawk on the telephone pole
almost at eye level,
its carvings of feathers, its brightness
unruffled by all the commotion
it caused in my simple yard.
Praise to my simple yard.
And praise to the telephone pole
far from forest and field
yet honored by this occasion;
to the bare branch of the oak tree
past which I could see so well

how the hawk sat without flinching
while a dozen oracular crows
teased it and dove; how it waited—
its huge calm, its attention—
then lifted its wings and rose
over my neighbors' roof tops.
Praise to the roof tops. Praise
to the squirrel scampering out.
And praise, too, to my heart

which forgot how it feels to look up
at the sudden, the unexpected,
and remembered today in an instant.
Praise! Praise to the hawk!

## Diligence

A nuthatch is hammering seeds
into the fence post. I heard it
when I opened the front door.

All day yesterday it kept flying
from the feeder to the trees and house.
At first I thought it was a neighbor
tapping in a nail. . . .

Now it's out there in the first cold
morning of the fall.
When I woke, before daylight,
the most disproportionate sadness
came over me,

the one that owned my life
for months last time until some bright
distraction flashed through the air.

Thank heaven another day of earnest
busyness is beginning in the leaves.

Sometimes I wake up
to a grief I can't remember
the cause of, which slips in
under my sleep, and which for days my mind
must have been working desperately to ward off.

## The Best Hour

*On reading that morning is the best time
for human procreation*

Morning: the perfect hour for making love—
when the body wakes refreshed to greet the body
stretching to meet it from its artless slumber.
Could we have been mistaken after all
these years of simply waiting it out for darkness
so we could rush upstairs? Think of the hours
we've wasted dressing quickly, eating breakfast,
before day whisked you off. Think of the bees
coupling in broad daylight in the shrubbery
while we were pulling weeds or washing windows
to finish in time for lunch. Not that the sunset
moving across your shoulders wasn't lovely,
or the moonlight on the sheets or on the grass,
but thirty years of thinking it accidental
that sometimes, rolling over, just at dawn,
we'd tangle with abandon, still half–dreaming,
half in the world, half out, desirous
and surprised to be so yielding quite so early. . . .
Luckily I was in your path those mornings
you took fire like the trees the sun had touched.

## At the Corner of the Eye

In Science, years ago,
the teacher assigned homework:
study the night sky,
wait till a star flickers
at the corner of the eye,
then turn to face it squarely
and see it disappear.
I watched, amazed: stars glittered
and vanished, reappeared
just as I turned away.
They were the herons rising
over the field the day
I searched for tadpoles, watching
the blue sky of the pond,
then saw it pulse with wings.
Or they were someone's face
half–glimpsed, a look I'd longed for,
that vanished when I looked.
Or they were something else:
a vision, seen askance,
that flickered in the mind,
an unexpected light
I turned to recognize,
then looked for all my life
and never saw again.

## In the Backyard

This morning a hawk plunges
straight for the squirrel at my feeder
and leaves only
its signature: blood on the snow.

All morning it circled the yard,
then dove, stunning itself
on the glass sky of my window,

and in minutes returned, braving
the thin, perilous channel
between hedgerow and house. I was watching
its path as it fell, its persistence,

and the squirrel, how it dashed
for the downspout, finding itself
motionless under the heat
of the hawk's body,

the claws in its rib cage, the sudden
tearing of wind as it rose
over the fence, the feeder,

the tops of maples and houses.
All morning it stays with me, not
the squirrel's terror, the hawk's
accuracy, but only

how it must feel to be lifted
out of your life, astonished

at the yard growing smaller, the earth
with its snow–covered fields tilting,
and what must be your shadow
flying across it, farther
and farther below.

## Sickness in July

All day I heard my neighbor's mower start
and stop. Squirrels clattered
in the eaves beside my bed. Along the wall
light drained from gold to mauve. My hand lay
like someone else's, limp and motionless
for hours, on the quilt.

                    When you turned on
the radio, downstairs, I might have stood
in a room of strangers who knew each other well.
Their conversations, the day's news drifted
beneath me while I floated far above
a language I didn't know. . . .

## Monet's Garden

*"I perhaps owe having become a painter*
*to flowers."* — *Claude Monet*

Rainy afternoons
the blues blurred
into each other.
He strolled through
brush strokes: irises
against sky, ponds
filling, a bright
canvas still wet.
Now that he had
flowers to paint
on rainy days
at Giverny, no day
would be wasted.
When sun filled
foxgloves, the bold
cups of red poppies,
he rearranged the effect.
Lifting anemones, moving
nasturtium nearer
the path, he saw how
everything spilled
over: wild
geraniums poured
into lilies, puddles
of pink saxifrage, waves
of gold grasses. Dissatisfied,
he scraped off the spent
blossoms, added
masses of starry dahlias,
smudges of briar roses

in slow wind. Daily
he "dug, planted,
weeded . . . evenings
the children watered."
The picture was never
finished: always a new
vista emerged—leaves
shifting, purple
fading to silver, the rose
ripening. Alone in the house,
pleased with the raked
paths, he watched rain
making its alterations.
His hand followed
quickly: columbine
dried in the left
foreground, asters
lifted their bowed heads.
As light became color, sky
vanished behind
foliage, no surface
remained bare. Even
as Camille died, he began
"focussing on her temples—
graded colors which death
was imposing—they were
blue, yellow, grey tones. . ."
like storm coming over
the garden, like
evening without crimson,
without sienna. At last

there was no horizon, only
a dense canvas painted
to great depth. It was
everywhere: blur
of children or leaves, paths
flowing away through
lindens, his own hand
vanishing as he reached
for a blossom and touched
azure: skies, oceans,
that sea spreading
over him as he sank
into it, into the deep,
inescapable garden.

*Flurries*


Out mowing I look up
from grass into a light
so unexpected I can't
name it. Snow flies
up through the oak's
bare branches, sifts
through brown tatters
of birds' nests, floats
toward heaven. As if
clouds had nothing to do
with this brightness, I keep
mowing: *the last
time,* I tell myself, sleeves
whitened with flakes, thinking
how wonderful, thinking
how deft and successful
summer was—telling
its story, making so much
grass, such a rich
language of bees, leaves,
birds, I had almost forgotten
this whirling, this wild flying
of everything back into
silence, the swarm
of winter.

## Blizzard

Snow falls in the night. By noon,
when the fence has vanished, I wade
through snowdrifts, lifting the feeder
to a nail over the porch.
The maple that held it sags
over snow, like a heavy skirt.

At dinner the roof creaks.
Drying the plates I imagine
tunnels of ice and the snow
piling against windows. At night
I read late, with excitement,
as if someone I love were about to visit.

## Annunciations

*"A slight sound at evening picks me up by the ears
and makes life seem inexpressibly serene and grand.
It may be in Uranus, or it may be in the shutter."*
                                    —*Thoreau's JOURNAL*

It may be
that the ledge of ice
sliding from the roof
is the world's crust
cracking, letting us
see out,
or that the bees
humming in the wall
are voices of the kind
Mary heard
when the wind lifted
its wings softly
and she knelt, simply
to still her trembling
knees.

                    *


Or it may be
that the thin language
of the leaves is not
calling you at all,
even if your ear
quivers with importance
as the trees murmur
back and forth, back
and forth all evening, only
to themselves.

                    *


14

Sometimes the light
shifts suddenly, causing us
to look. We notice
the radiance of the old
chair. Eager
for messages,
we interpret this
as a sign.

*

It may be.

Which is why, this evening,
when the walls of my grief seemed
impenetrable,
the cardinal on the wire
called me out,
though of course it didn't
and was talking only
to someone like itself.

*

Anyway,
I happened to overhear.
And now the stars
are lighting up the maple,
and anyone might believe
this light was intentional
as if it were sent
light–years ago
to move toward tonight
like a gift.

*

And tonight,
in my yard,
it may be.

II

## Early Morning Fog

Every morning my neighbor's house
reappears behind the back fence.
Today there's nothing, not even
the fence.

          From my kitchen window
I can see the porch steps fading
into fog. Farther off, the lilies
have disappeared, leaving only
the tall, luminous white one.

I was planning
to stake it today, but now
I walk about aimless
and a little awkward
in the empty rooms.

I keep noticing the lily. . . .

Even when I don't look
it's there
          floating

disconnected
from its stalk.

*Intruders*

Late in the night, a sound
under our window: leaves
or a scudding step. . . .

                       I don't
ask what you make of it,

asleep as you are, your face
turned from the path of moonlight.

I know
something has come for us.

                  *

In the morning I find proof
in the compost: the rotted orange
I left there last night, missing.

Whatever arrived, I asked it
without knowing.

                    Tonight,
carefully, I leave nothing.

                  *

And on the news
we hear of a fox sighted
on Maple, far
from river and woods, surrounded
by traffic and tall buildings,

and of the homeless who sleep
unseen in our yards, borrowing
porches and unlocked cars.

I wake in the night, thinking
I hear whining, the door
of the car opening, closing. . . .

You sleep soundly, and when
I wake you, you hear only
a branch scraping the awning.

I've heard stories: how bears,
searching for territory,
arrived in a suburb and raided
garages and open cellars,

*

and it may be
that this too is a place
that was taken from them.

## The Raccoon

Just as I drop
a jar in the trash can
she dives up, eyes
glittering, claws

clutching the rim
of terror, and goes
over, the can
with her, glass
crashing, things

breaking apart
everywhere and
not a thin moment
too soon as she darts
through the safe channels
of evening, and I

rush to the house,
breathless, hands
gripping the door,
slamming it, plants
spilling from sills,
everything wild,
clattering.

## Guests

A spark flies to the porch,
then to the hollyhocks, then
into the trees. . . .

At dinner a guest
spoke of her son's suicide.

I remember her husband's voice,
how it rose over the silence
to cover some vague flaw.

Later, waving goodbye,
I saw how the night swallowed
their pale heads in the car.

Now they are on the freeway,
and we hold hands on the steps.

Only the dim porch light
marks where we are, the great
spaces of night reach us,

and the fireflies dance through them
into the ghosts of branches
and over the long, black fields,

unlike us, at home with the silence.

## Glass

I look out and your red coat
arrives as your tricycle
turns from behind a tree,
filling the window where only
seconds ago I was seeing
sky and our single maple
as always for years I saw it
with you in my arms, the leaves
falling as now when you seem
separate from me as a picture
taken last year. I want
to call you, but can't, as in dreams
I am voiceless and calling, pressing
my face against glass—a train
window, a subway. . . . Is this
how it will be: clear
sunlight, your face that I love
intent on the leaves as I stand
beyond sound, at the rim?

## Evil Song

Evil comes to me this morning
folded between the weather
and the sports page, in the yard.

I open it, forgetting
it is often there, and look
in the pit of Evil's face.

I will give it to no one else
by naming
its inventiveness,
its newest manifestation,

but it stays with me
in the car, in the supermarket,
singing, *Suffering, suffering. . . .*

What good have I done anyone
to keep it so in mind?

And how dreary
my song will make the world.

I go out to my garden
and busy myself, grateful
for the warm September sun.

I know why I'm out here
again, watering, watering. . . .

I've seen how that phlox leans
carefully out of the shadows
as far as it can
and as long.

## The Toad

The toad enters my mower—
such a hard
slicing! such a sleek cut!

There he lies,
his head hinged
like a flap,
his slick legs

motionless as I take him
out to the compost heap,

remembering
how the car just ahead of us
plunged through the guard–rail,

the girl's hand
found last, deep in the woods,

and we drove home
without speaking,
passing familiar places,

entering separately
the small world of the spared.

## Crossing

Crossing the street I felt
a car pulling me with it, wind sucking
my coat, it was so close.
Back on the sidewalk I thought
*wait* before every step, bristled
at shop windows, at blades
of voices, the killer–doors
glistening as I flowed
into them, into the aisles
of cosmetics and jewelry, the clerk
asking if she could help. It was
the voice of the first nurse
after surgery, or the sun
reaching a room where windows
darkened like walls. I could only
accept, and how grateful I was
for suggestions: a scarf,
a bracelet, the clear
light from the corridor, something
to reach me, something to show me
the way out.

## The Power Failure

Rain battered at the house
with a violence all evening; wind
tore at the trees. . . .

Earlier my anger
ripped across a room
hitting you, the only
object in its path.

But when the lights went out
I called to you,

and you had lit a match
so I could find you
at the bottom of the stair.

This morning
when I woke, you'd gone to work,

and in the sodden yard
I checked for damages: a few
drooping peonies, nothing
irreparable.

Then I saw the huge limb
torn from the maple—

I wonder if you noticed.

All day
it's been lying there
like a heavy animal
in the relentless light.

I can't lift it, I can't
coax it away. . . .

*There—*


Plunging my hand
through thick leaves into
clear well water,
I imagine a day
when leaves fall from our maple,
so many I can't see
the hole in blue air
but feel my hand
go through, to the other side.

## When the Light Shifted

All morning I pulled weeds
from the perennials, avoiding
hanging out the wash.
Now sheets sag on the line,
and the sun has left the place
where they might have bleached and dried.

It leans over the porch
and the kitchen window with its row
of half–ripened tomatoes—
a frost has killed the vine.
Only the blackened stalks remain outside.

Those weeds would have disappeared
in a week if I had left them
to the cold October nights.
But today, in the backyard,
what I wanted was distraction,
as if something vague
and irreparable could be made right—
the way that bird keeps tugging at a red string
in my laundry basket, though it isn't
nesting time. . . .

## Black

At evening the first headlights
appear on the black road. Black trees
rise at my kitchen window, black
leaves drift slowly down. It is as if
grief is in everything. Black hair,
black dress, they have put you
into the black earth. Why must the night
match this, the color of such emptiness,
stroke by black stroke? Why
do I watch the car, hoping it turns in or
that the driver, dim in a faint light,
will wave, motioning me from the dark?

## The Fox

Snow creaks underfoot.
In the clearing the pond
smolders, its white smoke
motionless while the sun
pales, plunges
down, down into the deep

river of evening. I walk
slowly, lifting the cold
weight of my body which feels
nothing, thinking
*so this is the way grief*
*numbs to oblivion,* when

suddenly over the rim
of fences, a fox flares
in the distance, the last sparks
of light igniting its hot
fur—and my face, hands, even
the roots of my hair steam
helplessly, reddened
with wildfire.

## At the Storm Door

This morning a plate of ice
slides from the roof. I notice
icicle prints in the snow.

It's March. Finches and jays
rally around the feeder.
I must have filled it myself,

wading in heavy boots.
"Put one foot before the other,"
a friend said to me once

when my will froze.
I see now what she meant:
that ice—slide in a rush,

then jays seeding the snowbanks.
I must have known this could happen
last week, knee—deep in the drifts.

III

## At a Window

In the green half–light
of maples
we gather in the kitchen,
still predictable
as any family scene:
the young sprawled out
as if the room's too small
to hold them,
and the elders, still
solicitous and careful,
pouring milk.

But one of us
already moves away:
the son
glancing at a window
where leaves sail past
on the first winds of September
though it is summer here,
and soon the daughter,
her cheek already
brightened, a crimson leaf. . . .

Only we remain
unequivocal this morning,
printed in shades of light.
Soon we too
will seem awkward
in our old costumes
till light bleaches us
whiter than thin curtains
at a window
which gradually disappears
into the snow.

## All Weekend

Rain ripped hard through the oak
and sheeted the grey windows.
I heard its endless rapping
from each room of my house.

Outdoors the wax begonias
floated beyond the lettuce,
and lemon–lilies flattened;
huge peonies sagged and broke.

I tried to read. In Tolstoy
too it was still raining,
and on the evening news
I watched the coast guard rescue

a woman from a roof top
in Maine where it had rained
for weeks: the streets were rivers.
I studied the survivors.

By Sunday night, in bed
and half–asleep, I drifted
anxious and solitary
in a small, unanchored boat.

## Wearing My Son's Shirt

Looking for something to wear
in the garden, I put on
my son's oversized shirt. I feel
like a soul trying on a body.

This one's too large, but I like
the coolness of breezes under
my collar and cuffs. I like
believing that I can expand

in any direction. Just now
I was billowing, buoyant, a flag
flapping over the melons. I thought
*birds' wings,* but it was the shirt

trailing in parsley. I feel
like my son must, coming out
on the porch, seeing someone wearing
his shirt, unsure who I am.

## New England Asters

Let's be practical—

after August when the phlox
have faded and the shasta
daisies lie in tatters, what
remains

      if not these tall
ubiquitous first cousins
near the fence?

        All summer
I forgot about them in their drab
ambiguous green
like neighbors on vacation,

but yesterday
I thought I saw them coming, yesterday
I sensed a certain coolness
from the coast,

        and here they are:
this one pink and rosy, this one
crimson and effulgent
with a yellow eye,

Alma Potschke and September Ruby
spilling through the yard
in early morning,

wild, yes, but punctual—

all the way from Massachusetts.

## Jogging in the Cemetery

No sign saying, *Don't run*.
Nevertheless I slow down
to keep pace with the dead
who move with great effort.
I can hear their bones

pulling themselves together
as they catch on.
I can tell how they take notice.
They consider the wet streets,
maples ablaze, shops

open across town.
They remember their lit rooms
and thick sofas. They try
shaking the dream off,
the dream in which they are dead

and somebody jogs past.
I feel how they mean to run
with me in this middle–aged
morning, amid gravestones,
in the mild sun.

41

## The Ordinary Life

A friend writes, "You won't know me;
I have chosen
the ordinary life. . . ."

Reading this I remember
the secret we once shared:
how we lived for the rare moment
when light burns inward
and the small knot of self
dissolves in a flare of leaf,
the brief, unexpected bird
splitting the sky open.
To have chosen the ordinary—
as if comfort were common
or order could be expected
when over the rinsed plate
or a daughter's unbrushed hair
a star suddenly flickers
on the familiar wall,
when curtains are visited
by odd, unpredicted gusts,
and we look up during dinner
at a face known but unknown.

Even here, in unmapped rooms,
a tangle of vine thickens,
and a bird cries, sudden
and changed in a foreign country
through whose unfamiliar paths
we arrive home.

## After the Ice Storm

When I go out
the oak glistens.
Chandeliers sway
over me,
crackling
in the brisk golds
of the sun.

Now the pond steams
by the road,
blue light
arcs from the downed
power line just ahead,

and a jeweled nest
spills, crashing
through cracked lenses
of maples. Everything

that has stayed sealed
all night in its own silence
wakes to this, eager
to let go, to break
through the starred voltage
and fall

shattering, as amazed
as I am to come alive
on the charged path,
so faceted, so
invitingly dangerous.

## At Zero

Ice forms in the eaves.
All night the boards of the attic,
creaking like boxcars.

The pillow is cold, the sheet. . .
I float on the frozen surface
of ponds, or a field in Russia.

You turn from me in sleep.
Your train, leaving forever,
crosses the border.

## At Your Father's Funeral

It's you who carry
his ashes to the grave
and stand beside your mother.
I'm the one who holds

your other arm and hears
the first geese overhead.
They'd tell us winter's over
in another context,

insist we look away
past snow toward something warm
which reaches us. Remember,
in summer, how we planned?

And yet it's us I'm seeing:
one of us standing where
the last snow trickles off
the roadside, geese returning

in the air, and one of us
no longer here, as if
that wild blue sky did not
exist. What shocks me is the way

I never saw it, quite
how real the world would be
to one and not the other: how
it feels to walk away

with half your body, wings
in one ear and the other
soundless. In one eye,
the sun; the other, darkness.

## Spring Snow

This is what I asked for, something
fragile as crocus, lighter than blown cloud.
I wanted to look out and remember winter
a last time, and then go on with my plan
of greeting the first leaves, but with some regret.
After all, at the end of April, who can believe
the old rumor of frost? I want to recall
all summer the deep whiteness of that sleep
like a cool hand on my forehead while I wade
through the green jungles of August, while I lie
in the grass, in the thick heat, as the crickets start.

## Reunion

This must be the place
none of us planned on
the place we were going
when the doors to our lockers
slammed the last time
and we took off waving
in Chevies and Plymouths
straight into summer
and graduation
the streets of the town
blurring and morning
arriving like years
on our crumpled dresses
the walls of our houses
gleaming and children
born to us riding
away in their cars
fading and leaving us
facing each other
here where it seems
we've nearly come back
to our lives

## After Gardening

The last seeds have been planted,
and a shadow has fallen, over
the long rows. In the loose shingle
the wrens in their tiny nest sing
when the mother comes with their food.

Tired from planting, I'm lying
in the soft grass, listening.
I recognize the dove, the purple finch,
and the cardinal's *What cheer, cheer, cheer.* . . .

I want to rest here and savor
the first evening of summer,
its delicate green musk. All winter
I looked out my window as if at a blank page,
planning the story of flowers.

Now the ruffled blue iris
joins the poppy with its frivolous orange heart
and the black scar at the center.
I can hardly remember
how I woke in the nights and wept

over something unchangeable.
This year, for the first time,
I noticed the early crocus without elation.

But now the habitual tasks
have carried me out here: weeds
and the work of planting have left me
in the last natural light,

a light I can still see by.
Overhead, in the thin branches,
strands of the day are wound
with the pink threads of the evening,

and nearby, on the fence post,
a thrush is singing, busy with its life.

# IV

*The Flowering Trees*

## The Magnolia Trees

I have been walking
among magnolias
whose white stars
bloom all night, all day.

The wind blows them
about the evening
where they chart no courses
and guide no ships.

But if I were lost
I would like to follow
these bright blossoms,
these constellations

with the ways of clouds.
I think they could show me
the right direction
and if such lightness

were still possible.
And if it were not,
I would walk anyway
in these starry fields,

and rest a little
in my heavy body,
and let my mind
drift where it will.

## The Pear Tree

Nothing ever comes
of this tree, not
fruit, for the squirrels
steal it before

it ripens, not
shade, for its dead wood
was cut out, leaving little
else, certainly not

beauty, its sparse blossoms
comical near the oak.
And it gives so much
we don't want: sharp

spears scraping
the siding, a bridge
the raccoon climbs
to our chimney,

and in September the acrid
odor of rotting fruit.
Nothing
can recommend it. Still,

we keep it because
it's old, or the blade
of the axe is too dull,
or we wonder

what would we do
with the wood. . . . But I think
we keep it because
we remember a time

much younger, the house
heavy with heat
and anger. A breeze
came, and we found ourselves

in the yard, surprised by a gold
globe in the cool
darkness, and reached up
together, eager

to take it, the juice
spilling from tongues and fingers,
and nothing had ever tasted
so sweet, so good.

## The Shadblow Trees

Suppose you had done something
that was unforgivable.
Suddenly your life
runs like a black river

away from everything
and is so heavy with stones
it can never flow far enough.
Then you see the trees

ahead on the riverbank,
waving white flowers
as though they welcomed you.
They are only doing

what trees must.
But something in you
leaps and waves back,
something tells you

you could not have come here
without being called.
Of course the riverbank
will be different a week from now,

just another green face.
But although you are bringing
your sorrow with you,
you know you can live.

In so much fullness
you feel you could bear anything,
and if someone asked now
you would not turn away.

## The Crab Apple Trees

Once I wanted
a crab apple tree
to plant in my own yard.
It was the season

of apple blossoms,
and wherever I walked,
along the fences,
beside the ponds,

there were too many choices:
just when I came
to the one I wanted
I saw another—

red, lavender, white,
and so many shades of pink,
upright and weeping. Oh,
I was wild to have them,

and so I ran
from this one to that,
wanting them all: the ruddy,
the slender, so many names

and faces. And then
just before summer I came
to the one with the name I would give
to my child, Katherine. The season

of apple blossoms
had ended. Now when I walked
I no longer knew where I'd seen
that flash of brilliance, that branch

igniting a hillside, that sudden
snowfall beyond a roof.
Now there was only
a green haze

on the landscape.
When summer had nearly
passed, and the crab apples
were forming in every tree,

I found them again: there were clusters
of scarlet or gold, and they made
such a feast for the birds arriving
from every field. I saw

how the jays craved them—the sweetest,
the ripest—and how
I envied the birds flying
from tree to tree

searching: their bright
bodies, their dizzying lightness,
their wild, astonishing hunger
not yet filled.

## The Hawthorn Tree

Every April
the chance is given.
You have only
to walk out

through these green halls,
on these moist carpets.
You have only
to put out your hands.

Even if frost
still seals your eyelids
and your feet drag
in the heavy mud,

you can smell the fragrance,
you can find your way.
And if it happens
that your heart carries

a dark spike
at the center,
there is still the hawthorn—
once it was only

a cage of nails.
But the sun is beginning
its bright friction,
and the path ignites:

there is the tree
flaming with flowers
and the sun wheeling
with its shining keys.

## The Plum Tree

I was watering the new
plum tree in the garden when
you left your body. How
could I have known?

And when
they called, my hands were still
stained with soil and water.
I was planting

the plum tree
when you spilled
out of the world.
At times I think,

when I am busy, *Who
is leaving now?* Or,
*Who is lonely?* If
I knew I could abandon

anything. . . .
But usually I think
of how the phlox are spreading,
how the trillium

are thriving near the oak,
or else I weed
all day in the deep groves
of the lemon–lily to forget

myself. How could it be
that you, too,
were forgotten? Now the trees
are flowering, the plum

sends out its first
immaculate pink blossom
and the birds
have found it. It provides

a small diversion, still
so tenuous among
the maples and the more
protective trees.

## The Dogwood Trees

The dogwood comes back
drifting
its fine haze
through the hills.

And as if that were not enough
the rhododendron
bends down under the weight
of blossoms, the azalea

bursts forth. The hills
must be growing dizzy
with such profusion,
such wild, ponderous

cargo. I walk
first one path and then
another, thinking
of miracles, those

too in small gardens
and fields, even
in crags where nobody looks.
Sometimes my eyes

won't take any more, the sun
too brilliant, the trees
wavering as they mist
into each other. I close

my eyes, trying to press
into memory all
that could vanish, the green
leaves taking over,

falling. . . . I wish
this old habit
would leave me, the one
of looking at each joy

sideways to know
how to hold it, instead
of riding the bright waves
of the seasons, of taking

whatever gift has been given,
and then,
like the small trees of the hillsides,
letting it go.

## About the Author

Patricia Hooper is the author of *Other Lives*, which received the Norma Farber First Book Award of the Poetry Society of America, and of two children's books. Her poems have appeared in many magazines, including *Poetry, The American Scholar, The Hudson Review, The New Criterion,* and *Ploughshares.* She was educated at the University of Michigan, where she earned Bachelor and Master of Arts degrees, and lives in southeastern Michigan.